KINGFISHER KNOWLEDGE

DANGEROUS CREATURES

KINGFISHER KNOWLEDGE

DANGEROUS CREATURES

Angela Wilkes

Foreword by
Steve Leonard

KINGFISHER
BOSTON

Editorial director: Miranda Smith
Publishing manager: Melissa Fairley
Coordinating editor: Caitlin Doyle
Art director: Mike Davis
Consultant: David Burnie
Picture manager: Cee Weston-Baker
Production controller: Debbie Otter
DTP manager: Nicky Studdart
DTP operator: Primrose Burton
Artwork archivists: Wendy Allison, Jenny Lord
Proofreader: Sheila Clewley
Indexer: Sylvia Potter, Sheila Clewley

KINGFISHER
a Houghton Mifflin Company imprint
222 Berkeley Street
Boston, Massachusetts 02116
www.houghtonmifflinbooks.com

First published in hardcover in 2003
First published in paperback in 2007
10 9 8 7 6 5 4 3 2 1

1TR/1206/TWP/MA(MA)/130ENSOMA/F

Wilkes, Angela.
    Dangerous creatures / Angela Wilkes.—1st ed.
       p. cm.—(Kingfisher knowledge)
    Summary: Describes various kinds of dangerous animals such as
lions, piranhas, killer bees, and vampire bats.
    1. Dangerous animals—Juvenile literature. [1. Dangerous
animals.] I. Title. II. Series.

QL100.W56 2003
591.6'5—dc21   2003040063
ISBN 978-0-7534-6120-4
Printed in Singapore

GO FURTHER . . .
INFORMATION PANEL KEY:

 Web sites and further reading

 career paths

 places to visit

NOTE TO READERS
The Web site addresses listed in this book are correct at the time
of going to print. However, due to the ever-changing nature
of the Internet, Web site addresses and content can change.
Web sites can contain links that are unsuitable for children.
The publisher cannot be held responsible for changes in Web site
addresses or content or for information obtained through third-party Web sites.
We strongly advise that Internet searches should be supervised by an adult.

Prelim images: fat-tailed scorpion (1);
juvenile bald eagle (2–3); gray wolf (4–5)

Contents

Foreword

Working as a vet, I have encountered animals such as large aggressive dogs and the odd crazy cat, but they were nothing compared to the dangerous creatures I met while filming around the world: lions, Komodo dragons, poisonous snakes, and many more. But are these animals as deadly as we all think they are? Well . . . yes and no. In the right circumstances you can get quite close to many dangerous creatures with very little chance of getting hurt. I have picked up scorpions with their toxic sting and have not been injured because I was shown how to handle them properly. There are lots of ways of handling poisonous snakes so you won't get bitten, but the best way is not to pick them up at all! Most animals are aggressive toward humans only when threatened.

Some animals are dangerous because they see humans as food. Creatures such as lions, crocodiles, and big snakes kill and eat thousands of people around the world every year. If an animal becomes too dangerous, it has to be moved or killed. With more and more people on the planet there is less space for these animals. Magnificent beasts, such as tigers, are being forced into even smaller areas so that they will not be a threat to the human population.

Sometimes accidents happen. I have certainly had a few! The worst was while filming sharks in South Africa. Many people are frightened by sharks, but they are not as terrifying as people think. They may look like vicious man-eaters, but they rarely attack humans. Sharks have an excellent sense of smell to help them find prey, and also to taste their food before they devour it. I was diving in the sea surrounded by lots of little sharks that were looking for something to eat. One decided to nibble on my leg to see if I was worth eating. Sharks' teeth are very sharp, so it had no trouble biting through my wet suit. It was busy chewing on my leg when I spun around and punched it on the nose. The shark swam away. It was not trying to eat me—my leg would have disappeared very quickly if that was the case—but just find out what I was. It was all over so quickly that I did not have time to feel really frightened.

Working with dangerous creatures has taught me to respect them and to try to understand them more. I feel very privileged to have entered their world, and I want others to understand that these creatures need protection from humans much more than we need protection from them.

Steve Leonard—veterinary surgeon and presenter of the BBC TV show *Ultimate Killers*

CHAPTER 1

Tooth and claw

Predators have to kill other animals in order to eat. Many of them will also attack or kill other animals in self-defense or to defend their young or their home territory. In order to hunt successfully, predators have very sharp senses. Piercing eyesight, an acute sense of smell, and an excellent sense of hearing enable them to track down their prey. But just as important are a predator's body weapons—the fearsome tools it uses to catch and kill its prey.

Large carnivores, such as bears, big cats, wolves, sharks, birds of prey, and crocodiles, all have a formidable array of physical weapons. Razor-sharp teeth, daggerlike claws, and ferocious beaks equip them to tackle animals that are almost as big as themselves. These predators are not only strong, but they also can often move at great speed or use stealth to track down their prey. This makes them very dangerous to humans.

grizzly bear

Deadly weapons

All predators, no matter what type of animal they are, need fierce and powerful weapons to catch and kill their prey. Large predators, such as big cats and eagles, hunt large, fast-moving animals. It is vital that they are able to bring their prey down and kill it quickly before it has a chance to escape.

Each one of these efficient predators has evolved its own specialized set of body weapons, including ferocious fangs, long, hooked claws, or a fierce beak. These lethal weapons are pointed and razor sharp and are used for the initial kill as well as for tearing apart the prey's flesh afterward.

▲ Eagles and other birds of prey kill animals with the long, curved claws, called talons, at the tips of their toes. They attack their prey feet first, swinging the talons forward as they swoop down from the sky. The victim is caught in a vicelike grip by both the toes and talons and is either crushed so it cannot breathe or stabbed to death with the daggerlike back talons.

▶ Big cats, such as this lioness, are armed with powerful jaws and fierce teeth. Cats clamp their teeth around the neck or throat of their prey to suffocate it. The cat's long, fanglike canine teeth stab, rip, and tear through their victim's flesh. The smaller teeth at the front of the mouth nibble off meat, and the large, sharp teeth at the back of the mouth can slice through tough gristle and crack bones.

Built for speed

The cheetah hunts fast-moving prey such as gazelle, which live in open grassland. It does not pounce on its prey but stalks it instead, staying as low to the ground as possible, and then sprints forward and gives chase. A cheetah can cover 23 ft. in a single bound and can maintain a speed of 43 mph for several miles, swerving this way and that as the prey tries to dodge it. It can reach an astounding top speed of 70 mph, but it can only keep this up for a few hundred feet before its energy runs out.

▲ The largest and heaviest of all the big cats, the tiger is a night hunter. It tracks down smaller animals such as deer and wild pigs. Tigers do not usually hunt humans but occasionally they do become man-eaters.

Stealth and speed

Cats are masterful hunters and bring down their prey with a lethal combination of stealth, speed, and strength. Most cats—from the tiger to the domestic tabby—are solitary hunters and operate in a similar way: they stalk their prey, slinking forward slowly and silently, and then rush ahead and pounce, sinking their teeth into the prey's neck. Even the heaviest cats, such as tigers and lions, can leap with great power and agility.

The cheetah, however, is different. This cat runs rather than leaps and has developed the body of a true sprinter, making it the fastest land animal in the world.

Long tail held out behind the cheetah helps it keep its balance

▶ Unlike the other big cats, the cheetah has narrow, doglike paws with special paw pads to help it run fast. Its nonretractable claws help the cheetah keep a good grip on the ground as it sprints along.

The cheetah is smaller and slimmer than all other big cats. It has a strong but lightweight skeleton with long, slim legs. Its extended, flexible spine works like a spring, powering its huge leaps across the ground and enabling it to turn and swerve to keep up with its prey. The cheetah's skull is small and light, and its eyes are spaced far apart so that it can focus on its prey's movements. Unlike other cats, cheetahs do not have sheaths over their claws and cannot retract them. Like running spikes, they give the cheetah a good grip on the ground. Its long tail acts as a rudder, helping it stay balanced while it twists and turns.

Stealthy hunters

The other big cats cannot run fast over any great distance, so they rely on stealth, rather than speed, to catch their prey. They stalk the target as closely as possible before retreating from safety and then spring in for the kill. This demands both strength and agility since the cat usually pounces onto its prey's back before sinking its teeth in. Most of the big cats hunt animals that are smaller than they are because they hunt alone. The only exceptions to this rule are lionesses. They hunt in a family group, so they can bring down larger prey, which they share among the pride.

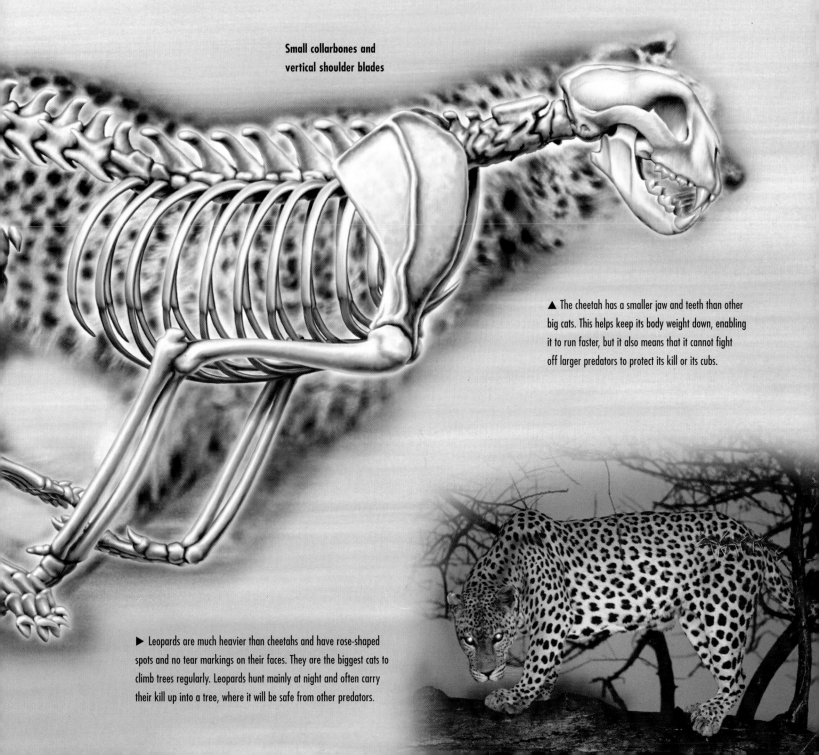

Small collarbones and vertical shoulder blades

▲ The cheetah has a smaller jaw and teeth than other big cats. This helps keep its body weight down, enabling it to run faster, but it also means that it cannot fight off larger predators to protect its kill or its cubs.

► Leopards are much heavier than cheetahs and have rose-shaped spots and no tear markings on their faces. They are the biggest cats to climb trees regularly. Leopards hunt mainly at night and often carry their kill up into a tree, where it will be safe from other predators.

A hungry polar bear tears a seal carcass on the sea ice. When food is plentiful, experienced polar bears eat only the seal's blubber and skin and leave the flesh. Younger bears and arctic foxes will finish the grisly remains of the carcass.

Mighty carnivores

Polar bears can weigh up to 1,368 lbs. (600kg) and are the largest land predators in the world. Not only are they huge, but they are also powerful swimmers and can run faster than reindeer over short distances.

Polar bears roam the sea ice along the coastlines that border the Arctic Ocean. They mostly hunt seals, not only on the ice but in the water, where they also attack walrus and white (beluga) whales. Seals swim below the ice but come up for air at breathing holes. A polar bear will lie in wait by a breathing hole and attack the seal when it comes to the surface.

Death blow

The polar bear kills a seal with a mighty swipe of one of its giant front paws. Then it hauls the seal out of the hole and rips it apart with sharp teeth. If a polar bear sniffs out a seal's birthing den hidden beneath the ice, it rears up on its back legs and then drops down on all fours onto the roof of the den, smashing through the sea ice to reach the baby seals below.

Massive strength

Despite their lovable image, bears are savage predators. They hunt alone and rely on their enormous strength to catch and kill large animals. A bear's strength comes from its size, weight, and sheer muscle power. Usually bears avoid contact with people, but they are very dangerous if taken by surprise—especially when they are with cubs or feeding from a kill. But bears are not the only large animals to fear. Giant plant eaters, such as elephants and hippopotamuses, are also strong because of their size and can be very dangerous if they feel threatened.

A charging elephant can run at speeds as fast as 25 mph. It is also strong enough to knock down any trees in its way.

A grizzly bear usually only rears to its full height of more 6.5 ft. if it is curious about something and wants to have a look around. However, a show of aggression means that the bear has been taken by surprise and is probably very frightened.

A grizzly end

The grizzly bear is regarded as one of the most dangerous animals in North America. It is big enough to kill a moose and can break the neck or back of most large animals with a blow from one of its huge paws. It can charge at speeds of up to 40 mph (64km/h) and is also an excellent swimmer. The grizzly bear is also skilled at fishing. It stands in the shallow water below waterfalls and catches salmon as they leap upstream on the way to their spawning grounds.

Giant plant eaters

Elephants and hippopotamuses are not predators—they are plant eaters. In Asia, however, many people are injured or killed each year by elephants raiding farmland to feed on crops. Bull elephants, especially Asian ones, also have periods of aggressive behavior called "musth" (or "must") during which they try to establish dominance over their rivals. At times like these they can be unpredictable and dangerous.

In Africa the hippopotamus causes more deaths each year than any other large animal, including the big cats. In rivers, such as the Nile, male hippopotamuses have areas called territories that they guard fiercely. They are very aggressive toward each other and will attack small boats that invade their territories.

Teamwork

Some predators hunt in teams—even though they are capable of catching prey on their own. A team has a higher chance of a successful kill than one animal working alone, and a team can bring down larger prey. Working as a team is also safer because it means that there are more eyes looking out for other dangerous predators. Each member of the team might end up with slightly less food once the spoils of the kill are shared, but hunting in this way ensures that the group as a whole has a greater chance of survival.

▼ A Cape buffalo (or African buffalo) is too large and dangerous for a lioness to tackle on her own. Four lionesses have chased this buffalo into a deep swamp from which it cannot escape and are moving in for the kill.

▲ African hunting dogs are thin and lightly built but have incredible stamina. This means that they are able to pursue prey over long distances.

Stalking tactics
Lionesses work in small groups to hunt large prey such as wildebeests (gnu) and zebras. When approaching a herd, they spread out in a line and move forward slowly, stalking, and then freeze, crouching. When they are within 6.5 ft. (20m) of the herd, they single out a victim and start the chase. One lioness leaps onto the prey, and the others quickly close in.

Family packs

African hunting dogs (also called African wild dogs) are perhaps the most efficient team hunters of all. They can bring down the largest prey in relation to their body size, and four out of every five hunts are successful. The dogs live in close-knit family packs of up to 20 adults and their pups. They hunt together and share catches with the whole pack, including the young.

The hunting party sets off at dusk. African hunting dogs hunt gazelles and antelope and sometimes wildebeests and zebras, too. They pinpoint a weak animal and then form a semicircle around it and chase it relentlessly. They can run at a steady speed of 25 mph (40km/h) for up to 3 mi. (5km), and they torment their prey by taking turns to snap at its sides and rear. When the prey gets tired, the dogs drag it down with their teeth and tear it apart.

A pack of wolves can bring down prey as large as a moose or a bison. Up to 30 wolves make up a family group, which patrols and defends its own hunting territory. Wolves mostly hunt caribou and other deer. When they have found a herd, they dart at the animals to find out which ones are old or weak before giving chase. Sometimes they encircle the prey and then close in. Other times they run the prey down, or one group drives it into an ambush set up by the rest of the pack.

▶ Wolves share the kill among the entire pack. The first share goes to the leaders of the pack— the alpha male and alpha female—and the senior hunters. Less active members of the pack and young pups have to wait until last.

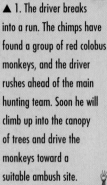

Killer chimps

Deep in the rain forests of West Africa chimpanzees will often group together to form teams of savage hunters. Their favorite prey are red colobus monkeys, and they hunt them with ruthless cunning and skill. Each one of the chimps has a specific role to play in a complex hunting strategy—either as a driver, a blocker, an ambusher, or a chaser.

▲ 1. The driver breaks into a run. The chimps have found a group of red colobus monkeys, and the driver rushes ahead of the main hunting team. Soon he will climb up into the canopy of trees and drive the monkeys toward a suitable ambush site.

▲ 2. A blocker takes his position in a tree. His job is to cut off the monkeys' escape route. He makes sure that he is sitting in full view of the fleeing monkeys and then bares his teeth fiercely and screams loudly. This frightens the monkeys and sends them running straight ahead toward the final trap.

2. Blocker

4. Ambusher

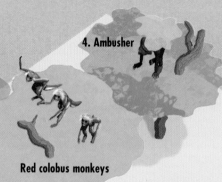

Red colobus monkeys

2. Blocker

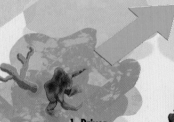

3. Chasers

1. Driver

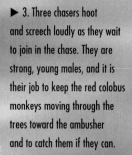

▶ This scene shows the chimpanzees' hunting strategy. Each member of the hunting team is in position, and the chasers are closing in for the kill. The red arrow indicates the direction of the chase.

▶ 3. Three chasers hoot and screech loudly as they wait to join in the chase. They are strong, young males, and it is their job to keep the red colobus monkeys moving through the trees toward the ambusher and to catch them if they can.

The chase

The hunt begins when one of the chimps, the driver, springs up a tree in order to separate some of the monkeys from their group. He then drives them toward the place where the other chimps are setting up their ambush. The blockers climb into the trees on each side of the ambush site and make sure they are easily visible. The ambusher rushes ahead and finds a place to hide. Now the chasers join in. They leap up into the trees after the monkeys and chase them toward the ambusher's hiding place.

▶ 4. The ambusher, usually the oldest and most experienced member of the hunting team, waits silently and concentrates on the chase from his hiding place among the leaves.

The kill

Now it is time for the ambusher to join the action. With the chasers on their tails and the blockers on the sides, the desperate red colobus monkeys are heading right into his trap. At exactly the right moment the ambusher jumps up in front of them, and the panic-stricken monkeys have nowhere to turn.

Sharing the spoils

The chimps either tear the monkeys apart up in the trees or carry them down to the ground, where the rest of their group are hooting with excitement. The senior members of the group take most of the meat, but if there is enough to go around, other chimps also get a piece. Quiet at last, but with bloodied hands and faces, the chimpanzees can now feast on their spoils.

Danger from the skies

For small animals danger can come literally out of the blue. Not only are they hunted by predators on the ground—a threat can also come from the skies. Birds that hunt other animals are called birds of prey. They are also known as raptors, from the Latin word *rapere*, meaning "to seize." Eagles, falcons, and hawks are birds of prey that hunt by day. Owls, on the other hand, hunt at night.

All predators need special equipment in order to hunt successfully. Birds of prey have highly developed senses to help them locate their victims, powerful wings for giving chase, and razor-sharp talons and beaks for executing the kill.

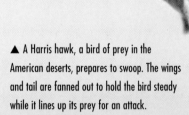

▲ A Harris hawk, a bird of prey in the American deserts, prepares to swoop. The wings and tail are fanned out to hold the bird steady while it lines up its prey for an attack.

Night hunters

As the sun sets owls set off to hunt. Some fly low over the countryside looking for prey, but others choose a high vantage point such as a tree or a rock. Owls have enormous eyes that are specially adapted to see in the dark. They also have an acute sense of hearing and can pinpoint the sound of an animal moving in total darkness, as long as there is very little background noise.

Once it has located a mouse or some other small animal the owl swoops in for the kill. The prey rarely hears it coming. Owls can fly silently since their primary flight feathers have fringed edges that muffle the sound of air passing through them. The owl seizes the prey and then flies back to its perch to eat it.

Hunting in the sky

Each bird of prey has its own hunting technique. Most soar high up in the skies, scouring the ground for signs of movement. A bird of prey's eyesight is about eight times sharper than a human's, and a bird, such as a vulture, can spot—from the sky—a rabbit over two miles away.

Some raptors, such as the peregrine falcon, dive down from the sky to catch their prey, reaching speeds of up to 124 mph (200km/h). Others, such as the golden eagle, scoop up their prey. This bird soars in the sky until it spots a rabbit or small animal and flaps quickly, loses height, and flies in low from one side, taking its victim by surprise. All birds of prey catch and kill their prey with their deadly talons, swinging them forward just before the attack.

◄ Highly focused and with its legs and talons outstretched, a tawny owl drops down upon an unsuspecting field mouse. The owl holds its wings back to act as brakes as it comes in for the kill.

The kill

Many birds of prey carry their catch back to their roost or a favorite plucking post before eating it. Falcons, hawks, and eagles do not swallow their prey whole since it is usually much too big. Instead they hold their food down with both feet while they tear it apart. A bird of prey's sharp, hooked bill is not usually used for killing prey, but it is the perfect shape for tearing off limbs and ripping off strips of flesh. It works like a combination of a butcher's knife and a meat hook.

Most birds just rip the meat and insides from their catch, discarding any bones and fur. They usually pluck the feathers because they cannot digest them. The ground beneath a bird of prey's plucking post, or feeding place, is often scattered with feathers.

Owls are the only birds of prey that swallow their prey whole. After they have eaten their catch they sit very still while they digest the meal. Inside a part of the owl's gut, called the gizzard, the meat is separated from the prey's fur and bones, which the owl cannot digest. These are formed into sausagelike pellets that the owl coughs up once or twice a day. Pulling an owl pellet apart is a good way to discover just what the owl ate for its last meal.

▶ The peregrine falcon catches ducks and other birds, which it devours at its favorite plucking post. It starts eating the prey's neck after pulling out a few feathers and often removes the bird's head and wings.

▲ The Harris hawk is one of the few birds of prey that hunts in groups. Three or four birds gather on nearby perches and take turns to fly high and survey the surrounding countryside for prey. They then harass their victim or surprise it with an ambush.

Danger in the water

Crocodiles and their relatives—alligators, gavials, and caimans—are the largest living reptiles on Earth, and they are fierce predators. They lurk unseen in rivers, lakes, and swamps in hot, tropical countries, lying in wait for prey. Saltwater crocodiles, the biggest of all, live in the salty water of river estuaries or in the sea.

Crocodiles' huge, scaly bodies, giant jaws, and crooked teeth give them a prehistoric look, and in fact their ancestors date back 200 million years—to the time of the dinosaurs. The crocodiles' unique hunting skills have made them efficient predators and extraordinary survivors.

▲ Although almost 44 ft. long, this saltwater crocodile has made itself almost invisible to any nearby animals. It is lying almost completely submerged in the water, with only its eyes, its ears, and some of the scales on its back clearly visible.

Ambush and attack

Crocodiles and alligators eat a wide range of prey—from fish and birds to large mammals such as zebras and wildebeests. They rarely attack and kill humans but may do so if they feel that their territory is being invaded.

Most crocodiles lie in ambush since this saves energy and float near the shore of a river or lake, waiting for animals to come to the water to drink. As they lie partly submerged in the water they are completely camouflaged and can breathe, smell, and hear without being seen.

▼ A herd of wildebeests is drinking at the river when suddenly an enormous Nile crocodile lunges out of the water and grabs the closest animal in its jaws. Unable to tear itself free, the wildebeest is dragged into the water.

► An American alligator basks in the sun on a sandbank. It opens its mouth to help it stay cool, showing a frightening array of teeth.

Ripped into bite-sized pieces!

As soon as an animal comes too close a crocodile attacks. It shoots forward out of the water, clamps its jaws around the animal's leg or muzzle, and pulls it into deeper water to drown it. It drags the animal underwater and then rolls over and over, like a spinning top, to rip it apart. Large prey often die from a broken spine as they are spun in the water. Crocodiles have to do this because their jaws are not strong enough to tear off pieces of flesh, and they are not able to chew. Their prey has to be gradually ripped into bite-sized pieces that they can then swallow whole.

Weapons and armory

Crocodiles have two to three times as many teeth as humans—a Nile crocodile has 68 teeth, and an American alligator has 80—but they are short and cone-shaped rather than being especially sharp. A crocodile constantly grows new teeth, so if one tooth wears out or falls out, another one grows to take its place.

Despite their bulky appearance, crocodiles and alligators are fast and agile. Powerful tails propel them through the water and give them a burst of power as they surge ashore. Their leathery skin is reinforced with bony plates, called scutes, making it as tough as a suit of armor.

A crocodile's ears and nostrils close underwater, and a third eyelid closes across its eyes to protect them. Flaps at the back of the crocodile's throat stop water from entering its lungs when it opens its mouth underwater to tear prey apart.

◀ A young Cape fur seal (or South African seal) is flung 6 ft. up into the air after a rough blow from the shark's massive jaw.

▼ A great white shark breaches, leaping straight out of the sea in pursuit of a seal. Young seals are most at risk—more than 80 percent of all shark attacks are on young or baby seals.

Ocean hunters

The most feared creatures of the oceans are the big sharks and toothed whales. Sharks have a chilling reputation because of their speed in the water, their terrifying teeth, and their ability to sense even a small amount of blood in the sea from a great distance. Some sharks, such as the great white, have been known to attack people, but they usually only do this if they mistake them for prey. A big shark hunts fish, seals, and sea lions.

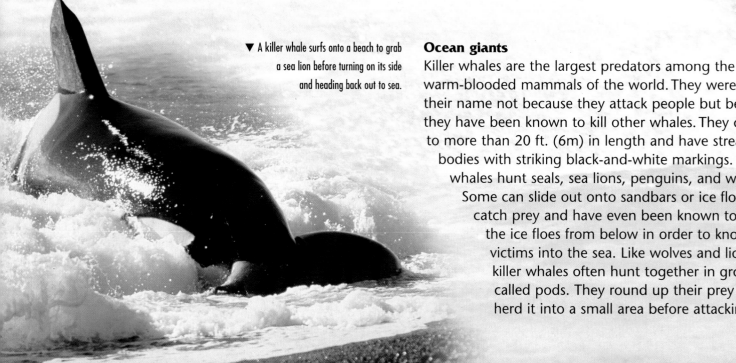

▼ A killer whale surfs onto a beach to grab a sea lion before turning on its side and heading back out to sea.

Ocean giants

Killer whales are the largest predators among the warm-blooded mammals of the world. They were given their name not because they attack people but because they have been known to kill other whales. They can grow to more than 20 ft. (6m) in length and have streamlined bodies with striking black-and-white markings. Killer whales hunt seals, sea lions, penguins, and walrus. Some can slide out onto sandbars or ice floes to catch prey and have even been known to bump the ice floes from below in order to knock their victims into the sea. Like wolves and lionesses, killer whales often hunt together in groups called pods. They round up their prey and herd it into a small area before attacking it.

Efficient hunter

The great white shark is considered by many to be the most frightening creature in the sea. Measuring up to 20 ft. (6m) in length, it has a sleek torpedo-shaped body and a powerful, crescent-shaped tail that propels it through the water at great speed. Its upper jaw is armed with triangular teeth with serrated edges that can slice through flesh, blubber, and bone. Its lower jaw is lined with long, pointed teeth that it uses to hold and slice through prey.

▶ Like all sharks, tiger sharks have tiny pits in their snouts. Special nerves inside them help the shark detect electrical signals given off by the muscles of its prey.

▲ Sharks are able to locate prey because they have a wide range of highly tuned senses that help them pick up the sounds and vibrations of other animals moving in the water. They can smell blood and other body fluids in the water from more than 0.6 mi. (1km) away, and the nerves in their snouts allow them to pick up tiny electrical signals given off by other animals. As the shark moves closer to a target it can sense changes in the movement of the water that help it home in on its prey.

In for the kill

The great white shark cruises along the seabed just off the coast in search of prey such as seals and sea lions. The shark is not really white but has a pale belly and a dark back, making it hard for prey in the water above to spot it against the ocean floor. The great white shark usually attacks from below. When it spots a seal, it shoots upward at speeds of up to 30 mph (48km/h). As it goes in for the kill its eyes roll back, and its lower jaw opens. From that moment on it relies on the electrical sensors in its snout to pinpoint its prey with deadly accuracy.

SUMMARY OF CHAPTER 1: TOOTH AND CLAW

Tooth and claw

This chapter looked at how the large carnivores attack and kill their prey. All of these predators are armed with fierce body weapons such as sharp teeth, powerful jaws, barbed talons, or a hooked beak.

Stealth, speed, and strength

The big cats use a combination of stealth, speed, and strength to catch their prey. Most of them stalk their prey and then pounce on them. The cheetah hunts fast-moving prey so it must chase at high speed. In fact, it is the fastest-moving animal on land. Bears rely on their size and strength to catch large animals. Polar bears hunt for seals, and a grizzly bear is strong enough to catch a moose. Large plant eaters, such as elephants, can also be aggressive and dangerous.

Teamwork

Some predators hunt in teams, giving them a greater chance of a successful kill. African hunting dogs and wolves hunt in packs, and lionesses work in small family groups to hunt large animals. Chimpanzees organize brutal hunting parties to catch and kill monkeys.

Lone hunters

Birds of prey, such as eagles, hawks, and owls, patrol the skies looking for prey. When they spot an animal, they swoop down and kill it with their outstretched talons and then tear the prey apart with their hooked beaks.

Crocodiles and alligators rely on ambush tactics. They lurk in rivers until an animal comes to drink and then lunge forward and grab it in their powerful jaws. They usually drown an animal before eating it.

Sharks and killer whales cruise through the oceans in search of prey. Sharks are highly sensitive and can locate prey from a long way away. Sleek and powerful, they attack at great speed and clamp their massive jaws around their target, ripping through its flesh with teeth like knives.

Go further . . .

Learn all about animals on the National Geographic Web site: www.national geographic.com/animals

For information on birds around the world, including birds of prey, visit the RSPB Web site: www.rspb.org.uk/international

For information on different types of sharks and shark conservation visit: www.sharktrust.org

Ultimate Killers by Steve Leonard (Macmillan, 2001)

The Life of Mammals by David Attenborough (Princeton University Press, 2002)

Zoologist
Studies animals and their characteristics and classifies them.

Primatologist
Studies apes and their conservation.

Ornithologist
Specializes in the study of birds.

Park ranger
This involves looking after nature reserves and parks. Experience as a volunteer will help you.

Wildlife photographer or camerperson
Photographs or films wildlife for books, magazines, or television programs.

Visit San Diego Wild Animal Park—known as the "zoo of the future"— where animals roam in herds and flocks over acres of land.
San Diego Wild Animal Park
San Diego, CA 92027
Phone: (760) 747-8702
www.sandiegozoo.org/wap

Visit U.S. National Parks, including Yosemite and Rocky Mountain National Park—one of the country's top wildlife-watching destinations. Go to: www.nps.gov for a listing of U.S. National Parks, including parks information, history and culture, and wildlife.

green mamba

CHAPTER 2

Venomous creatures

Some predators do not have the sheer size and strength to wrestle with their prey and kill it. They may also not have the right body parts—snakes, for example, have no limbs with which to hold onto their victim. Instead of fighting and risking getting hurt, these animals simply use poison. Their venom paralyzes their victims so that they cannot escape or kills them immediately. This gives the predator time to consume its meal leisurely.

Poisons are a complex mixture of different chemicals. Some animals, including many that use poison in self-defense only, have very powerful venom for their body size. Animals have different ways of injecting poison into their victims. Some have fangs; others use spines, stingers, or even hairs. All of these devices work like hypodermic needles, injecting venom directly into the bloodstream so it takes effect quickly.

Portuguese man-of-war

Venomous creatures

A huge range of animals—from snakes and spiders to giant jellyfish and tiny frogs—are poisonous. Animal poisons, often called venom or toxins, can be deadly chemical weapons. Some poisons just cause pain—others kill. Many animals only use poison for self-defense—to protect themselves from predators. Others use it to paralyze or kill their prey—because poisons act quickly, they are a very effective way to subdue fast-moving prey before it has a chance to escape.

Types of venom

There are two main types of venom. One affects an animal's nervous system, paralyzing the victim and leading to suffocation or a heart attack. The other stops an animal's blood system from working.

Venom is usually injected into victims using needle-sharp fangs, spines, or stingers, but it can also be in an animal's saliva or the slimy mucus covering its skin.

Killer tentacles

Jellyfish and their relatives ensnare prey in their long, trailing tentacles. Each tentacle is covered with stinging cells. As soon as the tentacles touch prey—or a person—poisonous darts shoot out from the stinging cells. These hold, poison, and paralyze the prey so the jellyfish can lift it to its mouth.

Injecting venom

Sea anemones and coral polyps catch
food in a similar way to jellyfish, but
many sea creatures use sharp spines
to inject venom into prey or predators.

Poisonous fangs

Many snakes, such as this eyelash
viper (right), are armed with poisonous
fangs. A snake's fangs are thin, sharp,
and curve backward, so it can get
a good grip on prey. Snakes strike fast,
jabbing their victims with their fangs
and injecting a strong dose of venom
into them. The venom of some snakes
is powerful enough to paralyze and
kill large animals. Spiders also have
a poisonous bite that they
use to paralyze or kill their prey.

Some poisonous animals are
brightly colored or patterned.
This warns predators that they are
dangerous and are best left alone.

▲ A king cobra lunges forward to attack in typical threat posture with its hood on display. It can hold itself upright with one third of its total length—over 6 ft. (2m)—and move forward with alarming speed, making a low, hissing noise like a dog's growl.

Feared snakes

Deadly venom, lightning speed, long, sinuous bodies, and flickering, forked tongues make people fear snakes more than most other animals. Many snakes grow several feet long and can swallow extremely large prey, making them even more daunting. Poisonous snakes do not hunt people but use their venom to immobilize or kill the small animals that they eat such as rats or lizards. They only bite humans to defend themselves when they feel threatened. Some snakes' venom is so powerful that it can kill a person if they are not treated quickly.

▼ The Gaboon viper has a huge, 6-ft.-long body and lives in the tropical rain forests of western and central Africa. It relies on camouflage to help it catch rodents and frogs. It lies in wait on the forest floor, its vivid geometric markings making it almost invisible in the surrounding leaves. The Gaboon viper has fangs that are 2 in. long—the longest fangs of any snake.

Deadly poison

The inland taipan, the most poisonous land snake, has such strong venom that a full dose can kill a human within 45 minutes. In fact the taipan only lives in remote parts of inland Australia and is so rarely seen that at one time people thought it was extinct. The inland taipan's main prey are rats, which move fast and can be dangerous because they bite and scratch. This means it is vital for a snake to have strong venom that will immobilize the rats quickly before they can cause injury. The taipan's venom attacks an animal's nervous system, stopping it from breathing and causing paralysis.

Giant among snakes

King cobras are the largest venomous snakes of all and can grow up to 18 ft. (5.5m) in length. They live in the tropical forests of Southeast Asia and eat other snakes and lizards. When the king cobra feels threatened, it hisses, rears up, and spreads out its neck ribs to form a hood that makes it look more frightening. One bite from a king cobra is lethal enough to kill an elephant. In fact up to 36 people die from king cobra bites each year.

◀ The inland taipan rears up aggressively in its characteristic "S" shape, ready to strike and revealing its bright yellow belly. The inland taipan is not known to have caused any human deaths at all.

Fastest snake

Almost 13 ft. (4m) long, the black mamba is one of the most feared snakes in Africa. It can move faster than any other snake, slithering along the ground at speeds of up to 10 mph (16km/h), with its head held high. Despite its speed, its aim is quick and accurate. The black mamba often lives in termite mounds or hollow trees and hunts rodents, ground squirrels, and other small mammals. Unlike other snakes, which swallow their prey alive, it bites its victims and then leaves them to die before eating them. The black mamba's venom is very strong and attacks the nervous system of its victims.

▼ The black mamba is slender but very strong. In fact, it is not black but a metallic grayish-green color. It might get its name from the color inside of its mouth, which is purplish-black. Just two drops of its venom can kill a person.

Poisonous fangs

All snakes are meat eaters, but they have no limbs with which to hold down prey and no teeth with which to chew it. Instead many snakes are armed with lethal poisonous fangs. These work similar to hypodermic needles. They inject poison into prey and paralyze or kill it. This gives a snake time to swallow its prey whole, safe from the danger of an active victim's sharp teeth or claws.

▶ A rattlesnake opens its mouth wide to strike and then sinks its two long fangs into an animal. As it does so venom is squeezed out of the venom glands and along tiny tubes, called ducts, into the snake's hollow fangs. The venom is then forced out of small openings in the fangs and injected into the deep puncture wounds that the fangs have made. It enters the victim's bloodstream instantly and is so powerful that it takes effect right away.

Heat-seeking snakes

Pit vipers, the family of poisonous snakes that includes rattlesnakes, cottonmouths, and bushmasters, have the most sophisticated fangs and detection devices of all snakes. They have heat sensitive pits or hollows on the sides of their faces that pick up infrared heat given off by nearby prey. This means that pit vipers can pinpoint prey in total darkness without being able to see at all. Pit vipers rely on ambush tactics to catch their prey. They strike with lightning speed, inject their venom into their prey and then often wait five to 30 minutes for the venom to take effect. Even if the prey manages to escape, it is too weak to go far, and the snake soon tracks it down.

Poisonous cocktail

Snake venom is like saliva or spit—but with a potent mixture of deadly chemicals. Each type of poisonous snake has its own type of venom, depending on the chemicals in it. A rattlesnake's venom mainly affects a victim's blood system. A snake's venom does not just subdue or kill its prey. Like saliva, it starts to dissolve and break down the snake's food as the first step of the digestive process. Snakes can control the amount of venom they inject so that they do not waste any. Although they do not need to eat as often as mammals, it can take a while to replace their supply of venom. Snakes are in danger from predators during this time.

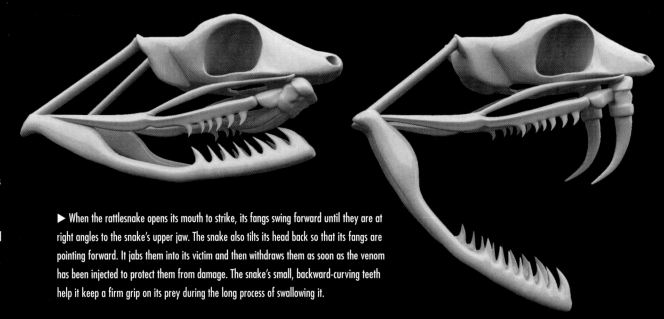

▶ Normally a rattlesnake's long, slender fangs are folded up flat against its upper jaw on each side of its mouth. This stops them from sticking out of the snake's mouth when it is closed. The fangs are tucked into a sheath of skin to protect them and keep their points very sharp.

▶ When the rattlesnake opens its mouth to strike, its fangs swing forward until they are at right angles to the snake's upper jaw. The snake also tilts its head back so that its fangs are pointing forward. It jabs them into its victim and then withdraws them as soon as the venom has been injected to protect them from damage. The snake's small, backward-curving teeth help it keep a firm grip on its prey during the long process of swallowing it.

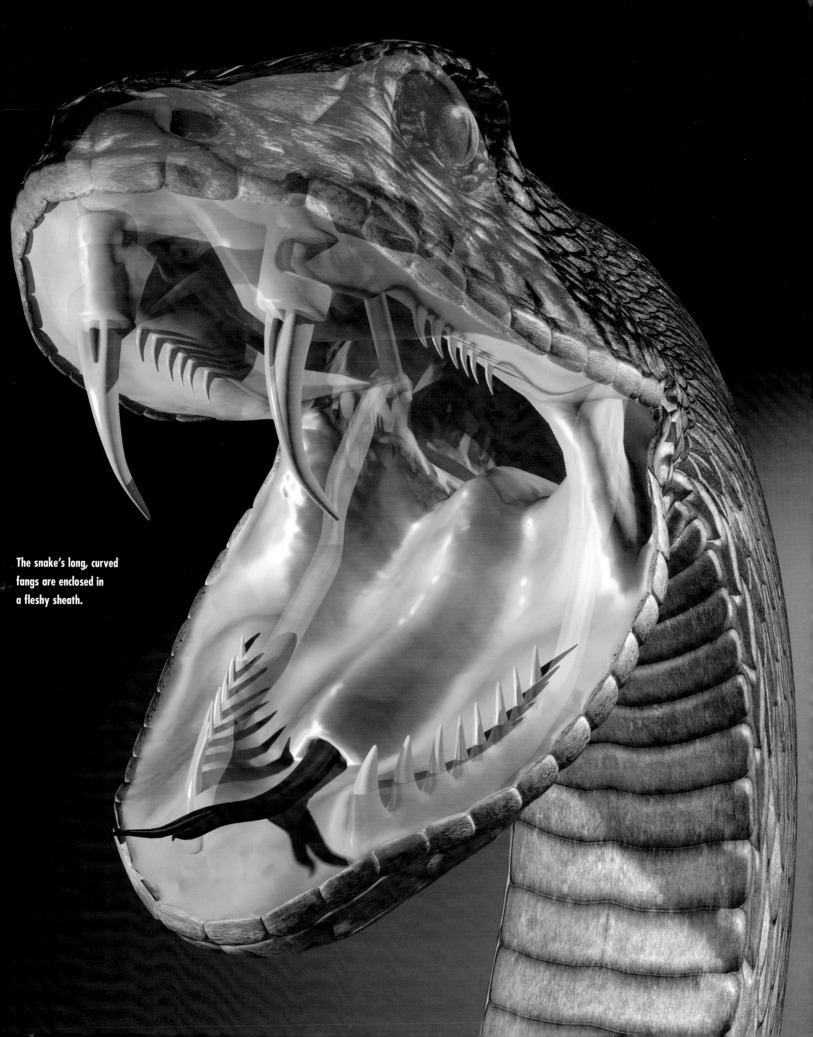

The snake's long, curved fangs are enclosed in a fleshy sheath.

◀ The golden poison dart frog is a close relative of the terrible dart frog—the most venomous frog of all. It is one of only three species of frogs that are toxic enough to produce effective blowgun darts.

▼ Strawberry poison dart frogs are named after their bright red skin, which is speckled with blue-black markings. These two frogs are peering over the rim of a bromeliad leaf high up in the rain forest canopy.

Venomous skin

Even small, harmless-looking animals can be deadly poisonous. Amphibians, a group of animals that includes frogs, toads, and salamanders, are born in water yet live on land as adults. They all have thin, moist skin through which they breathe—this skin can sometimes be poisonous.

The poison is produced by poison glands on the amphibian's back or scattered throughout its skin. The poison tastes bad and discourages predators from eating the amphibian. The most poisonous amphibians of all are very brightly colored. These colors act as a warning to predators that the animal is dangerous to eat.

Colorful frogs

Poison dart frogs, which live in the rain forests of Central and South America, secrete the most powerful skin poison of any amphibian. The poison is scattered throughout the frogs' skin and acts fast, attacking the nerve and muscle cells of a predator and causing heart failure. Poison dart frogs are so called because the Choco tribe in South America uses their poison on the tips of their darts. One frog produces enough poison for up to 50 darts. Poison dart frogs are tiny, only up to 2 in. (5cm) long, and come in many jewellike colors. These provide such an effective warning to predators that the frogs are active and can search for food by day, unlike other frogs.

The most poisonous frog of all, the terrible dart frog, produces up to 0.07 oz. of poison—just one tenth of which could kill a person.

▲ The enormous cane toad has a large pouchlike swelling on each shoulder. These are its parotid glands (near the ears)—big glands that produce toxins. More toxins are concentrated in the toad's warty skin, its muscles, bones, and body organs. The toad's eggs and tadpoles are also poisonous.

Poisonous toad

All toads have slightly poisonous skin that makes predators avoid eating them. The cane toad, however, is not only very large—more than 4 lbs. (1.8kg) —it is also very poisonous. Toxins are spread throughout its body but are concentrated in its warty skin and the two glands on its shoulders. When a toad is attacked, milky venom from these glands oozes into its attacker's mouth, causing heart failure, convulsions, temporary blindness, and even death.

Beetle control

Originally from South and Central America, the cane toad was introduced to Australia 60 years ago in order to try to keep beetles from infesting sugarcane crops, and soon spread rapidly. All of the predators of native Australian frogs, such as waterbirds and snakes, die from eating the toad.

Living in fire

The fire salamander grows almost 12 in. long and has a black body with yellow markings to warn predators that it is poisonous. Its skin produces toxins that taste terrible, irritate the eyes, and that can even kill small mammals. The salamander also has poison glands on its back and squirts poison in the face of persistent predators.

The word salamander means "lives in fire." People used to think salamanders could survive fires because they ran out of logs on campfires when they were lit.

▼ The black-and-yellow skin markings of the fire salamander are characteristic warning colors. Other color combinations that work in the same way are red and black and orange and black.

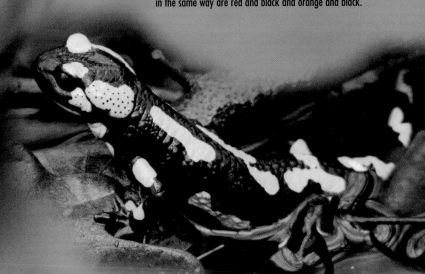

forked tongue

A deadly bite

Two completely contrasting types of lizards living in two different parts of the world have an especially harmful bite. They do not just use their sharp teeth to kill their prey—one has a poisonous bite, and the other has a mouth full of deadly bacteria. The Gila monster is a brightly colored lizard found in the southwestern United States. The Komodo dragon, a monitor lizard, lives on only a handful of small, isolated islands in Indonesia and is known locally as an "ora."

▲ The Gila monster has beadlike scaly skin that is black with pink-and-yellow markings. It has dark bands on its tail, a black face, and black legs and feet. Its bright colors probably warn predators that it is poisonous.

Venomous lizard

The Gila monster is one of only two poisonous lizards and grows up to 19.5 in. (50cm) long. It lives in the American deserts, resting underground in a burrow by day and coming out to feed at night.

The Gila monster feeds on eggs, nesting birds, ground squirrels, young rabbits, and any other small animals that live on the ground. It can only move slowly, so it relies on ambush tactics to catch prey. The Gila is not an aggressive lizard but will defend itself by hissing at and then biting anything that attacks it.

It has an excrutiatingly painful bite. The lower jaw contains venom glands, and when it bites, venom flows from these glands into grooves in the teeth. The lizard cannot inject poison into its prey or attacker, as a snake does, so it grips onto a victim fiercely and has to chew to work in the poison.

The Gila's venom affects an animal's nervous system, so it is useful for immobilizing prey. It is painful—and causes sickness and vomiting in humans, but is rarely fatal.

Mighty lizard

The Komodo dragon (below) is the largest lizard in the world. It can grow more than 6ft. (2m) long and weighs up to 442 lbs. (200kg). The dragon has no natural enemies on the islands where it lives and is a fierce predator, feeding on wild boar, deer, dogs, goats, snakes, water buffalo, and even humans once in a while. The Komodo dragon tends to hunt by ambush. It lumbers along forest trails, sniffing out prey with its enormous, flickering, forked tongue.

The Komodo can smell animals from as far as 3 mi. (5km) away and lies in wait for them in tall grass. Despite its clumsy appearance, the dragon can move very fast and charges out of its hiding place once prey comes too close.

A Komodo cannot keep up a chase for long, but even if it does not manage to hang onto the prey, it sinks its teeth in to subdue it. The dragon's breath smells foul since its mouth is full of poisonous bacteria. Even if the prey escapes, one bite is enough to cause a fatal wound. As infection sets in the animal weakens, slows down, and eventually dies. The dragon soon tracks it down again.

Moving in for the kill

The Komodo dragon's attack is ferocious and deadly. It pins its prey down on the ground with its powerful front legs and giant claws and then rips it apart. Like a shark, the dragon has bone-crushing jaws and sharp teeth with serrated edges that can tear through the toughest hide. The Komodo devours every morsel of its prey, including bones, fur, and hooves, ripping off large pieces of flesh and gulping them down whole.

◀ The giant Komodo dragon has all the trademarks of a predator. Its enormous size, powerful jaws, scaly, leathery hide, giant front legs, and lethal, long claws truly make it a daunting sight.

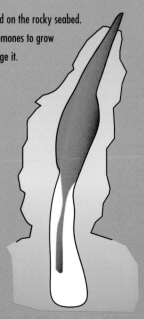

▶ A brightly patterned cone snail extends its proboscis toward an unwary fish. As soon as the snail makes contact a sharp modified tooth shoots down the proboscis like a hollow dart, stabbing the fish with a powerful venom.

◀ The puffer puffs itself up with water and raises its spines to scare off enemies and make itself hard to eat. Some types of puffers are poisonous—but only if they are eaten because their poison is concentrated in their internal body organs.

Underwater stingers

Danger lurks in unexpected places beneath the ocean waves. Many sea creatures have poisonous spines that they use to defend themselves from predators. Others, such as cone snails, use poison to catch prey. There are more than 50 different types of poisonous fish in the world's oceans. They make many people sick each year and have even been known to cause death. Some of these fish are almost invisible, lying camouflaged on the seabed. Others have bold, colorful markings to warn potential predators not to attack or eat them.

Hidden danger

The stonefish is possibly the most deadly fish in the sea. It lives on corals and rocks in shallow, tropical waters and relies on ambush to catch its prey. Its squat, warty body is camouflaged with splotches of color that make it seem invisible. The stonefish lies in wait until a small fish or crustacean comes close enough to seize and then swallows it whole.

The stonefish can hardly move and is unable to escape from predators, so it has a row of spines along its back that are tough enough to pierce sandstone. The minute the spines are touched or someone steps on them, they release deadly venom that affects the lungs and heart, causing suffocation or a heart attack.

◀ A stonefish lies concealed on the rocky seabed. It allows weeds and sea anemones to grow on its skin to help camouflage it.

▶ At the base of each stonefish spine is a venom gland. When pressure is applied to the skin covering the spine, venom shoots up a canal to the sharp tip of the spine.

◄ The long spines along a lionfish's back are disguised within frondlike fins. Each spine has a venom gland lying in a long central groove. If a lionfish is threatened, it swims toward its attacker with all of its dorsal spines pointing forward, ready to attack.

But these feathery fins contain an array of lethal poisonous spines—13 along its back, three beneath its tail fins, and two below its jaw. These spines contain poison glands, but the poison is used only for defense and never for hunting. Any predator trying to eat a lionfish is speared by the spines and is unlikely to survive. The lionfish's stripes warn predators that it is poisonous and that they should stay away. A person stung by a lionfish will suffer a lot of pain, convulsions, and breathing difficulties.

Deadly snail

Cone snails are tropical sea snails. Most species eat worms and other snails. A few, however, eat fish. Cone snails cannot move fast enough to chase fish, so they use poison to paralyze their prey.

The poison is delivered by a hollow dart. When the snail's snout touches a fish, it triggers a flow of poison. The dart in the snail's proboscis shoots out like a harpoon and injects the poison under pressure. Fish-eating cone snails are the most dangerous. They produce a nerve toxin that is strong enough to paralyze a fish within seconds or to kill a person. Medical scientists are currently researching the use of cone snail venom as a nonaddictive pain killer, which could be 1,000 times stronger than morphine.

Warning colors

Lionfish drift through the shallow, sunlit waters of tropical coral reefs, moving as close as they can to schools of small fish on which they feed. Lionfish are extremely beautiful, with gauzy striped and dotted fins that they hold up like fluttering fans. Their stripes help camouflage them against the background of the coral reef as they float waiting for prey.

▼ Sea urchins have sharp spines, but most are not toxic. The flower sea urchin, however, is very poisonous and dangerous.

Tentacles

Two of the most dangerous creatures in the sea are not armed with powerful jaws and sharp teeth but instead with trailing tentacles and deadly poison. The box jellyfish is the most poisonous sea creature of all and has toxins more potent than a cobra's. A person who has been badly stung can die within five minutes. Blue-ringed octopuses are tiny, yet more people in Australia die as a result of their bites each year than die from shark bites.

Danger in the water

Almost all jellyfish can sting, but most are not deadly to humans. When they do sting people, it is usually by accident or is just a self-defense reflex. Many jellyfish are carnivorous. The smaller ones feed on plankton, and the bigger ones feed on fish and crustaceans such as shrimps.

The box jellyfish, sometimes known as the sea wasp, swims near the coasts of northern Australia and Southeast Asia. Like other jellyfish, it pulses gently through the water, trailing its tentacles. It has 60 tentacles, each 9.8 ft. (3m) long.

The surface of each tentacle is packed with thousands of stinging cells called nematocysts. If hairs on these cells are triggered by contact with prey, they fire tiny barbed harpoons, injecting the prey with venom. Each nematocyst is tiny, but because there are so many of them, this can result in a huge amount of venom. One box jellyfish tentacle alone can kill an adult human.

◀ Box jellyfish have a pale blue translucent bell around 7.8 in. across. The bell has four distinct sides, hence the name "box jellyfish."

▶ During the jellyfish season huge swarms of jellyfish float out to sea, carried back and forth by the tides and currents. Moon jellyfish are common and widespread, but their stings are not powerful enough to harm humans.

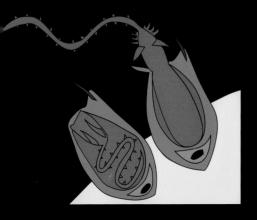

▼ Each nematocyst contains poison and a tightly coiled harpoon. When the harpoon is triggered, it shoots out of the cell very quickly, turns itself inside out, and sticks into the victim, releasing a shot of venom.

Once prey has been immobilized by the stings the jellyfish lifts it to its mouth using its tentacles. On humans box jellyfish stings cause agonizing pain and produce weltlike scars up to 0.2 in. wide. As with other jellyfish, even when a box jellyfish has died and its tentacles are dry, they can still sting if they come into contact with soft, wet skin.

Small but deadly

The blue-ringed octopus is tiny but deadly. It measures only 7.8 in. (20cm) across with its tentacles outstretched, yet the venom glands in its head contain enough poison to kill ten people.

▼ The blue-ringed octopus prefers to hide or flee rather than attack. Like other octopuses, it uses jet propulsion to swim, taking water into its baglike body and then forcing it out behind it to propel it forward. It makes its body as streamlined as possible to increase its speed.

The octopus lives in shallow waters and rock pools around Australia and some Pacific Ocean islands, where it hunts for crabs. Its tentacles are lined with suckers, but these are harmless to humans. It is the bite from the octopus that is lethal.

The octopus has sharp jaws like a parrot's beak. When it bites its prey or a person, it injects venomous saliva into the wound. The venom causes paralysis, heart failure, and death.

The octopus is normally a dull yellow color with pale blue circles, but if it is feeding, feels threatened, or trapped, its body color darkens, and the circles turn electric blue, warning predators that it is poisonous. Young blue-ringed octopuses do not have the blue rings and rely on squirting out clouds of ink to escape from predators just like other octopuses. Once the blue rings have developed, however, they no longer need to do this.

SUMMARY OF CHAPTER 2: VENOMOUS CREATURES

Venomous creatures

This chapter looked at the different ways that animals use poison to kill their prey or defend themselves. It also looked at how poisons work. Some affect an animal's nervous system, leading to suffocation or a heart attack. Others stop an animal's blood from flowing.

Deadly snakes

Poisonous snakes do not hunt people, but they do use venom to immobilize or kill the small animals they eat. Some snakes, such as the king cobra, have venom that is strong enough to kill an elephant.

Poisonous skin

Amphibians, such as frogs, toads, and salamanders, have poisonous skin to discourage predators from eating them. Their bright coloring acts as a warning to their attackers.

Dangerous lizards

Two different kinds of lizard, the Gila monster and the enormous Komodo dragon, are poisonous. The Gila monster has a toxic bite which causes sickness and vomiting in humans; the Komodo dragon has a mouth full of deadly bacteria which it chews into its victims, causing a slow and very painful death.

Poisonous sea creatures

Many sea creatures use venom to catch their prey or protect themselves from attack. The stonefish and lionfish both have poisonous spines that are used purely for self-defense. Cone snails, on the other hand, are slow-moving sea snails that use a powerful poison to paralyze their prey. Jellyfish have long tentacles, armed with thousands of tiny stinging cells, that they trail through the water. The tiny blue-ringed octopus has a deadly poisonous bite, making it one of the most dangerous creatures in the sea. The venom glands in the head of the blue-ringed octopus contain enough poison to kill ten people!

Go further . . .

For detailed information on animals, plus quizzes and printouts to color in, visit: www.enchantedlearning.com

Visit the National Aquarium of Baltimore's Web site for information on animals that live in the sea: www.aqua.org

Learn more about the Gila monster at: www.gila-monster.org

The Blue Planet by Andrew Byatt, Alastair Fothergill, and Martha Holmes (Dorling Kindersley, 2002)

The Natural History Museum Book of Predators by Steve Parker (Carlton, 2001)

Herpetologist
A specialist who studies reptiles and amphibians.

Zookeeper
Summer work experience at a zoo would help you find out more about the job.

Museum worker
Classifies species and prepares exhibits for display to the public.

Marine biologist
Specializes in marine ecology.

Television researcher
Does the background research for natural history television programs.

Visit the National Aquarium in Baltimore, one of the best aquariums in the world, and explore the collections of worldwide marine life.
National Aquarium in Baltimore
Baltimore, MD 21202
Phone: (410) 576-3800
www.aqua.org

Denver Zoo is one of the most popular zoos in the U.S. Here you will have the chance to see almost 4,000 animals—including the Primate Panorama and the Dragons of the Komodo Exhibit, as well as 144 endangered species.
Denver Zoo
Denver, CO 80205
Phone: (303) 376-4800
www.denverzoo.org

CHAPTER 3

Small but deadly

When people think of dangerous creatures, the first ones that come to mind are the large carnivores. Yet some of the tiniest creatures are just as frightening—and even more dangerous.

Many people squirm at the thought of creepy crawlies—and the sight of a scorpion with its tail raised or a large, hairy spider is enough to make anyone shake with fear.

Although many scorpions and spiders are harmless, some of them are very deadly. Other small creatures have become legendary for being lethal. Piranhas are famous for tearing their victims apart within minutes, and vampire bats are linked to legends of blood-sucking monsters that come out at night. In fact, the biggest killers of all are also the smallest. The mosquito kills millions of people each year by spreading malaria. Other insects spread many horrible diseases. These insects are all tiny, but they are responsible for many more deaths than sharks, crocodiles, or snakes.

Australian funnel-web spider

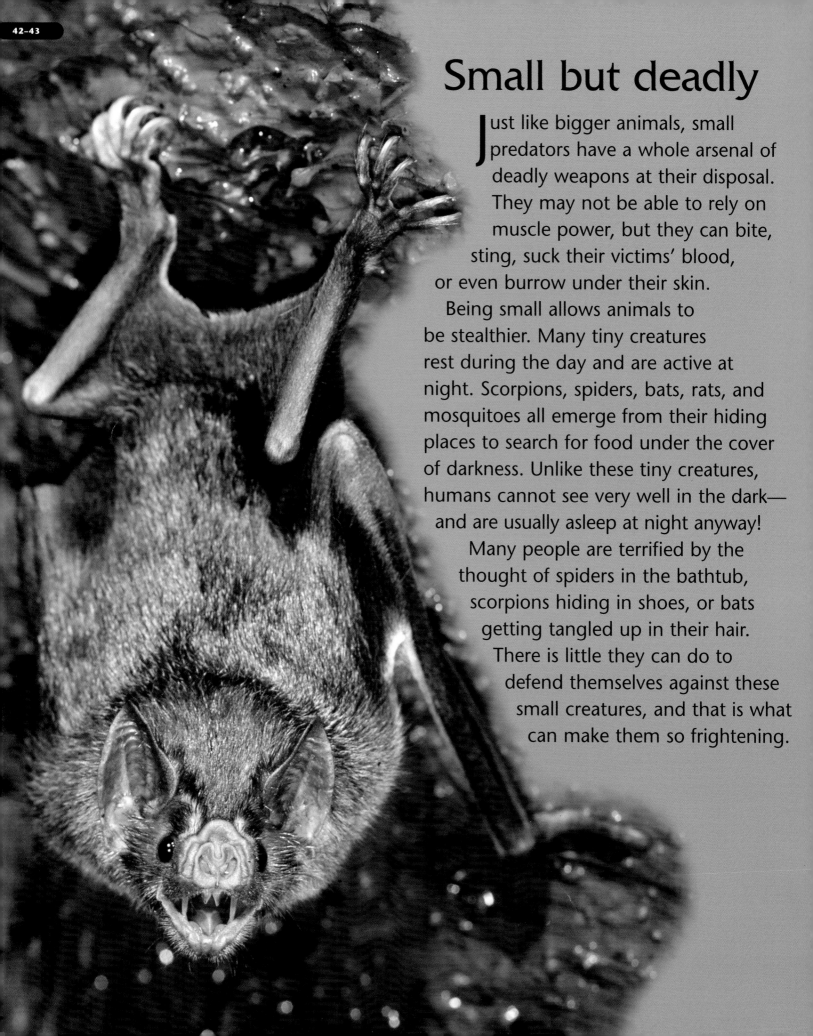

Small but deadly

Just like bigger animals, small predators have a whole arsenal of deadly weapons at their disposal. They may not be able to rely on muscle power, but they can bite, sting, suck their victims' blood, or even burrow under their skin. Being small allows animals to be stealthier. Many tiny creatures rest during the day and are active at night. Scorpions, spiders, bats, rats, and mosquitoes all emerge from their hiding places to search for food under the cover of darkness. Unlike these tiny creatures, humans cannot see very well in the dark— and are usually asleep at night anyway! Many people are terrified by the thought of spiders in the bathtub, scorpions hiding in shoes, or bats getting tangled up in their hair. There is little they can do to defend themselves against these small creatures, and that is what can make them so frightening.

Dangerous teeth

Animals do not have to be large to have a dangerous bite. Piranhas (right) are only 12 in. (30cm) long, but they are armed with powerful jaws and fierce teeth. One piranha on its own may not be able to kill an animal, but a school of piranhas can.

Vampire bats (left) use their razor-sharp front teeth to make cuts in their victims' skin so that they can suck their blood. Rats are equipped with amazingly strong teeth that can gnaw through most things.

Potent poisons

Many tiny creatures use venom to subdue or kill their prey or to defend themselves from attack. Spiders have poisonous fangs, scorpions wield a vicious stinger at the end of their tails, and bees use their venomous stingers as the ultimate form of defense. In some cases a spider's or scorpion's venom is stronger than that of a snake—a much bigger animal.

Spreading disease

Many insects, such as mosquitoes, tsetse flies, and fleas, are not poisonous themselves, but they kill millions of humans and livestock each year by spreading infectious diseases whenever they bite.

All of these insects feed on the blood of animals or people. Once they have become infected with a disease—as a result of feeding from an infected animal or person—they pass it on to any other creature they feed from. Small as they are, these insects really are deadly, and there is little that people can do to prevent them from spreading infections.

Sinister spiders

Many people are terrified of spiders. All spiders have a poisonous bite, and they use it to subdue or kill their prey. Most of the 50,000 or so species of spiders are harmless to humans, but a few are dangerous. Their bites can cause long-lasting wounds—and can even lead to death if they are not treated with antivenin promptly.

▲ The brown recluse spider, found in the United States, is just over 0.4 in. long. It looks harmless, but its venom is a lethal mixture of chemicals that destroy body tissue and cause painful ulcers that do not heal. The spider often bites people, but deaths are rare.

▼ A goliath tarantula sinks its large fangs into a mouse. To attack, it rears up and then strikes downward, injecting venom into its prey with fangs that are 0.4 in. long. Also known as gigantic bird spiders, they eat young birds that they drag from their nests.

Hairy giants

Goliath tarantulas (also called gigantic bird spiders or bird-eating spiders), the biggest spiders of all, have a leg span of 11 in. (28cm), so the largest are the size of dinner plates. They are found throughout South America in tropical rain forests and hunt small animals. Goliath tarantulas only bite people in defense as a last resort. If they feel threatened, they release a cloud of tiny barbed hairs that work their way into a person's skin and cause severe irritation.

Black widow spiders

The black widow is considered the most venomous spider in North America, with venom that is 15 times more poisonous than that of the prairie rattlesnake. In fact, like most spiders, the black widow eats insects. The female usually hides upside down in her web. When an insect gets caught in the web, the spider bites holes in its body and sucks out the insides. Only the female black widow is poisonous—the males and spiderlings are harmless. But the spider's bite is not usually fatal to humans because the spider injects only a small amount of venom. Black widows have this name because of the belief that the female black widow kills and eats the male spider once she has mated. This only happens occasionally.

▲ The Sydney funnel-web's fangs drip with venom when it is about to strike. Only 0.28 in. long, the fangs are enormous in relation to the size of the spider's head and are sharp enough to pierce the skull of a small animal. Only the male funnel-web's venom is harmful to humans. A toxic mixture of acids and nerve poisons, it is made in venom glands behind the spider's fangs.

▶ The female black widow is shiny black in color with a reddish hourglass shape on the underside of her abdomen. The male is only about half her size, with a smaller body and longer legs.

Funnel-web spider

The Sydney funnel-web is the most dangerous spider of all. Its fangs are strong enough to push through a fingernail, and its venom is powerful enough to kill a human—unless they are treated with antivenin quickly. The spider is found in the suburbs around Sydney, Australia, and the males often come into contact with people when searching for a mate. Like goliath tarantulas, the funnel-web rears up to strike so that it can stab its fangs downward. Its venom attacks the nervous system, paralyzing the muscles and causing severe breathing difficulties.

▶ A Sydney funnel-web spider hides in its web. As soon as an insect trips on one of the trip wires the spider attacks.

Cunning web

As the name suggests the entrance to a funnel-web spider's web is shaped like a funnel and leads down into a burrow lined with spider's silk. The spider also spins long strands of silk that stretch out from the entrance of the web—like the ropes that secure a tent. These strands act like trip wires. The spider hides just inside the entrance to its burrow, waiting for prey. As soon as a frog, lizard, or insect trips on one of the threads the spider feels the vibrations and rushes out of the hole to seize its victim.

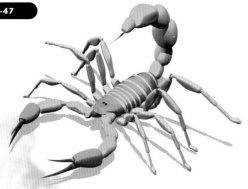

▲ When a scorpion feels threatened or is about to attack, it opens both of its front claws and raises its tail. A scorpion's tail is very flexible. It is made up of five separate segments with a bulb-shaped part, called the telson, at the end.

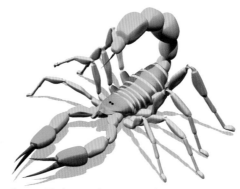

▲ If prey is difficult to grip, the scorpion carefully arches its stinger forward over its back to aim at a soft spot on its victim such as a joint. Each type of scorpion has venom that works on the animal it eats such as insects or crustaceans.

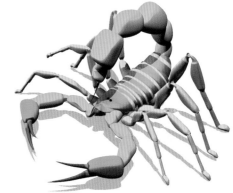

▲ The scorpion jabs its tail into the prey and injects a dose of venom. It rocks the stinger back and forth to work its way into the victim's flesh. Meanwhile muscles around the scorpion's venom glands contract, squeezing the poison through the hollow stinger into the prey.

Stinger in the tail

The sight of a scorpion hiding in a shoe or scuttling across the bathroom floor strikes fear into the hearts of most people. All scorpions are poisonous and, despite being small, some of them produce venom that is powerful enough to kill a person.

Scorpions are arachnids—so they belong to the same animal family as spiders, ticks, and mites. Like other arachnids, they have jointed legs, but they also have giant pincers and a segmented tail with a poisonous stinger at the tip. There are around 1,500 different types of scorpions living around the world—but only 25 of them are dangerous to humans.

Open claws show aggression

▶ At the tip of the fat-tailed scorpion's tail there is a swollen, bulb-shaped segment ending in a long, sharp, hollow spine. Inside the bulb are two venom sacs full of poison. Muscles attached to the base of the bulb move the sting backward and forward.

African fat-tailed scorpion

During the mating season male scorpions will often wander into houses searching for females. They find hiding places under beds and in other nooks and crannies.

Like all scorpions, the fat-tailed scorpion is a predator and hunts soft-bodied prey such as spiders, centipedes, cockroaches, beetles, and even other scorpions. It catches animals in its pincers and then stings the victim to stun it. Some scorpions have such powerful pincers that they can crush their prey and do not need to sting it. Small scorpions with weak pincers, however, use their venom so they can catch prey as large as they are.

Scorpions also use their stingers to defend themselves. The fat-tailed scorpion's venom is as strong as a cobra's, but the reason it is dangerous is that its tail is strong enough to pierce through clothes and even shoes. The scorpion strikes several times, so it is able to inject large amounts of venom into its attacker. It is thought to kill 250–400 people a year in Tunisia, in northern Africa.

Death stalker

The scorpion with the most potent venom of all is the Palestine yellow scorpion, sometimes known as the death stalker. It does not inject very much venom at a time, but the actual poison is much more powerful than that of a cobra. Found in deserts and other dry habitats in Asia, the Palestine yellow scorpion hides in small, natural burrows or under stones. Its venom is a powerful mixture of neurotoxins—poisons that affect the nervous system. Unless the victim is treated quickly with antivenin the scorpion's sting leads to coma, convulsions, and fever. The victim will usually die of heart failure or breathing difficulties.

▼ Unlike most other scorpions, the Palestine yellow scorpion has both slender claws and a narrow tail. Other scorpions have either huge claws or a fat tail.

Night prowler

Scorpions are thought of as desert creatures, but in fact they are found in several other habitats as well, from grasslands to rain forests. The African fat-tailed scorpion—the most dangerous scorpion to humans—originally lived in shallow burrows or under rocks in northern Africa. As its territory has become more built-up, however, it has moved into people's homes. It especially likes damp places, such as bathrooms, where there are lots of insects to catch.

▲ Piranhas only mount a serious attack when they are swimming in a school. They swim just below the surface of the water with all their senses alert for signs of movement or disturbance that might signal prey.

Fierce fish

Piranhas have the reputation of being the world's fiercest fish. Terrifying stories tell of people falling into the Amazon river in South America and being stripped of all their flesh within minutes, amidst waters swarming with angry fish. It is true that piranhas are armed with frightening jaws and sharp teeth, but of the 20–26 different species of piranhas only four may be dangerous to humans and even then only in certain situations. In fact, no case has ever been recorded of anyone having been killed by piranhas.

Tropical home

Piranhas are only found in South America, from Venezuela down to Argentina. They live in large, slow-moving rivers, such as the Amazon, that flow through the tropical rain forests into the Atlantic Ocean. Despite their reputation, piranhas have wide-ranging appetites. Most of them eat fruit and seeds, or take small bites out of the fins and scales of other fish, which soon grow back. The most dangerous of the species are the red-bellied piranhas.

▶ As with most animals the front teeth of a fish provide vital clues about what it eats. The red-bellied piranha has powerful, deep jaws, a flat face, and a mouth full of thin, triangular teeth as sharp as knife blades. These teeth can slice through an animal's flesh easily, each bite leaving a crescent-shaped cut about the width of an adult's thumb.

▲ The Amazon is one of the longest rivers in the world. For most of its length it is slow-moving and muddy, providing ideal conditions for piranhas. Many different animals live in the rain forests bordering the river. When they come to the river to drink, they may fall victim to the piranhas.

Underwater predators

Red-bellied piranhas are carnivores—the young piranhas eat insects and small crustaceans, while the adults eat birds, rodents and other mammals, frogs, and reptiles. Red-bellied piranhas are only dangerous when water levels are low and food is scarce—this makes them more aggressive. They are not scavengers and only eat fresh meat. Red-bellied piranhas are unlikely to attack strong animals moving steadily through the water. Instead they target weak, drowning, or wounded animals that are struggling and splashing.

In for the kill

Piranhas do not really work together as an organized team. Each fish works as an individual predator. However, being in a group means that the fish can attack much bigger animals, such as tapirs and capybaras, than they could on their own. If one fish is attracted by the splashes of an animal in distress and swims toward it, the rest follow. They gather around the victim, and the smaller fish dart forward to take a few small test bites. If they are successful, the older, larger fish join in, and they all take lightning-quick bites out of the prey.

A piranha's powerful jaws snap shut just like a mousetrap. It cannot chew, so it only uses its teeth to cut and bite and then swallows each mouthful of food whole. Red-bellied piranhas turn sideways in the water when they bite, revealing their gleaming red bellies.

If an animal becomes distressed when it is bitten, the piranhas go wild. They twist and turn in the water, biting so fast that the water looks like it is boiling. In a frenzy like this the piranhas can strip their victim of all of its flesh within minutes, leaving behind nothing but bare bones.

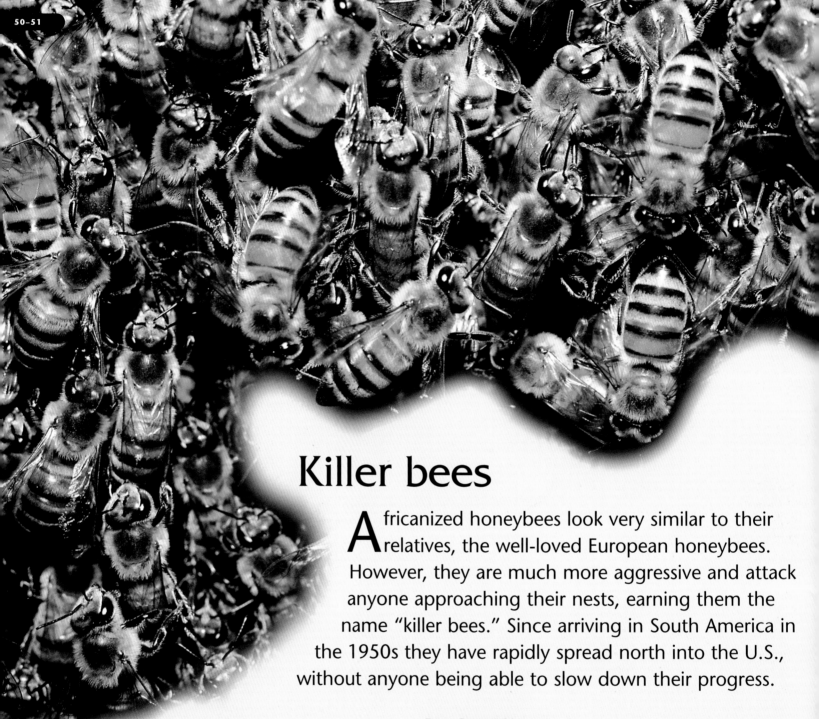

Killer bees

Africanized honeybees look very similar to their relatives, the well-loved European honeybees. However, they are much more aggressive and attack anyone approaching their nests, earning them the name "killer bees." Since arriving in South America in the 1950s they have rapidly spread north into the U.S., without anyone being able to slow down their progress.

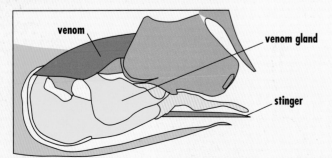

▼ A bee's stinger is made up of two barbed darts that are held together in a sheath and connected to a venom gland. When the bee stings, muscles push the darts deep into the victim's flesh.

venom

venom gland

stinger

Bees from Africa

Africanized honeybees, as their name suggests, are not native to South America. In 1956 a professor working at a university in Brazil took 63 queen bees from Africa to Brazil. He wanted to breed a new type of honeybee that could produce a lot of honey in the tropical climate of Brazil—and African honeybees had the most productive colonies he had found. Some of the queen bees escaped and bred with local bees, creating a new type of bee—the Africanized honeybee. These bees were similar in many ways to their African ancestors. They were aggressive and quick to take over the hives of local bees. Even more worrying, however, was that they were ferocious when it came to defending their hives—so much so that many beekeepers gave up bee-keeping completely.

◄ Like other honeybees, killer bees feed on nectar and pollen from flowers and produce honey from the nectar.

▶ Swarms of bees, such as this one in the eaves of a house, are less dangerous than nesting bees because they do not need to protect a hive or the growing larvae inside it.

The bees had very few natural enemies in South America, so they flourished in their new environment and began spreading. By 1986 they had reached Mexico, and now they have settled in the southern states of the U.S. as well.

Swarming bees

Like other honeybees, Africanized honeybees live in large colonies. Every once in a while a colony flies away to find a new nesting site. While waiting for a scout to find a good place, the whole colony rests on a tree or house in a huge mass called a swarm. European honeybees may only swarm once each year, but Africanized honeybees form swarms six to 12 times each year.

The bees often build their nests in man-made objects such as holes or cracks in buildings, under mobile homes, in sheds, or in log piles. This brings them into close contact with people. They build smaller nests than European bees because the climate is warmer and they do not need to store honey in their hives over the winter.

However, the bees attack and sting any person or animal that approaches their nest. Like other bees, they die as soon as they have stung something, so they sting as a means of defense only. The bees can chase for up to one third of a mile (0.5km). As each bee stings the attacker it gives off a warning scent calling other bees to join in the attack. Even bees from other colonies can join in, so there could be thousands of bees altogether. Each bee sting is no stronger than a bee sting from another species of bee, such as the European honeybee, but the number of stings is very dangerous, and they can kill a person unless they are treated quickly. Since the 1950s around 1,000 people have died from attacks by killer bee swarms.

▶ Africanized honeybees look very similar to European honeybees, but they are slightly smaller— less than one inch long.

Spreading disease

Some of the deadliest animals in the world are also the smallest. Many insects spread germs and diseases—ranging from food poisoning, a short-term illness, to real killers such as malaria and sleeping sickness.

Most diseases are caused by bacteria, viruses, or tiny single-celled creatures called protozoa. All of these things are parasites—this means that they feed and breed on other animals. Parasites need a way to move from one host animal to another—and when they do so, they spread disease. Many lethal parasites are carried from one host to another by insects.

▲ The common housefly eats any food that it can find, spitting on it to turn it into a soupy liquid that it can mop up. The fly breeds on animal dung, rotten meat, and vegetables. It can carry millions of harmful germs both on and inside of its body.

▲ Screwworm maggots take one week to mature on their host animal. By this stage they look like small screws, the reason for their name. When they are around 0.6 in. long, they drop off of their host and form pupae on the ground. Flies emerge within three days.

▶ When a female anopheles mosquito lands on a person's skin, she points her long proboscis at it. This acts as a sheath for tiny, pointed probes called stylets that sink into the skin and enable her to draw blood.

proboscis

▲ Fleas jump from one animal or bird and to another and feed by sucking their blood. Fleas can spread deadly diseases such as typhus. The bubonic plague, which killed millions of people in Europe in the 1300s, was carried by fleas living on black rats.

Body invaders

The female screwworm fly can lay up to 400 eggs in open wounds on humans and other animals. The eggs hatch into larvae that burrow into the host's flesh and feast on it until they become full-sized maggots. The maggots' saliva is toxic and makes smelly pus that attracts more flies to lay eggs. If the animal or person is not treated quickly, they become sick and die. In the past millions of cattle were infected with screwworm flies, but now they have been wiped out in many areas as governments have had sterile male flies bred to prevent the females from laying eggs.

► This tsetse fly is full of blood that it has just sucked from a human. If the fly is carrying a parasite, it can pass a deadly disease, such as sleeping sickness, on to every person it bites. The victim will think that he or she has the flu at first but will then become very sick.

Biggest killer

Indirectly the mosquito kills more people than any other animal by transmitting a deadly disease called malaria. There are 2,500 different species of mosquitoes, and they carry many diseases, but only the female anopheles mosquito carries the parasite that causes malaria.

Male mosquitoes feed on nectar from plants, but female mosquitoes feed on blood because they need the protein it contains to help them grow eggs. They can land on most parts of a person's body without him or her even realizing that they are there. If a mosquito has already drank blood infected with malaria, it infects more people each time it bites. This is because it injects a small amount of saliva into a person's skin when it bites in order to keep the blood flowing. Although malaria can be treated, more than one million people still die from the disease in Africa each year.

A deadly bite

The tsetse fly is part of the same family as the housefly. It is tiny, but it is still able to infect half a million people living in Africa each year— 80 percent of whom will eventually die.

The tsetse fly feeds on the blood of animals and humans. It often carries a single-cell parasite, called trypanosome, that works its way into the body and attacks the blood and nervous systems of its victims. In humans it causes sleeping sickness—a painful disease that ends in coma and death unless it is treated. Any human who is not treated for the disease then becomes a potential host for healthy flies. These flies become infected when they bite their human carrier and spread the disease even further.

In animals the tsetse fly causes a disease called nagana. This disease kills three million livestock animals each year, which has led to huge economic losses in 36 African countries—many of which are already desperately poor to start with.

Sadly, although sleeping sickness is quite easy to treat, the medicine is very expensive. The World Health Organization estimates that it costs around $31 million each year to fight the disease.

◀ Vampire bats find their way around in the dark by echolocation. They make tiny sounds that bounce off of objects in their flight path. The bats pick up the echoes that come back to them and use this information to pinpoint where things are.

Vampire bats

Simply mentioning vampire bats often conjures up nightmares. For centuries this small, blood-sucking bat has been connected in people's minds with myths about immortal beings wandering through the night to suck the blood of the living. In fact, the vampire bat feeds mostly from pigs, cows, and horses. The main threat to humans comes from the fact that the bat spreads disease.

▲ The common vampire bat has long, triangular incisors with sharp cutting edges. Using these, it makes a small wound around 1-in. (2.5-cm) deep in its victim's flesh.

Blood-sucking bats

Vampire bats are found in northern Mexico and South America. They are the only bats in the world that feed on the blood of other animals. They need to consume half of their body weight in blood every night, and they may die if they do not feed for two nights in a row. There are three types of vampire bats—the white-winged and hairy-legged vampire bats feed mostly from birds, but the common vampire bat feeds from mammals.

Common vampire bats are about the size of a mouse, with a wingspan of 12–14 in. They live in colonies—there are usually around 100 bats in a colony, but numbers can be as high as 2,000. The bats roost during the day and search for food at night, flying about three feet above the ground, looking for herds of animals.

▲ Vampire bats roost in caves, crevices, and trees. They hang upside down in tightly-packed groups, with the bats on the outside facing away from the center. The bats make a lot of noise as they fidget and groom each other.

Stealthy techniques

When it has found an animal, a vampire bat uses heat sensors in its nose to find a good spot to feed from such as veins close to the skin. Unlike other bats, a vampire bat can move backward and sideways like a spider, as well as run and jump. This agility makes it easier for it to attach itself to prey.

The bat snips off any fur or hair with its teeth and makes a cut in the animal's skin. It then sticks its tongue into the wound and laps up the blood. The bat's saliva produces anticoagulant—a chemical that stops the animal's blood from clotting and keeps it flowing. Another chemical in the bat's saliva numbs the animal's skin so that it does not feel anything. The bat feeds for up to 40 minutes. When feeding is done, it uses its strong back legs and thumbs to catapult itself back up into the air.

Vampire bats do not harm animals by draining them of their blood, but they do spread disease, especially rabies, which kills hundreds of thousands of cattle each year. Also—very rarely—they feed from people, who can also die from rabies. Another problem is that the anticoagulant in the bats' saliva prevents wounds from healing properly, which leads to serious infection.

▼ Vampire bats bite animals in places where it is hard to shake them off. They often feed from between the ears or eyes or on the neck, back, or shoulders. Humans are bitten on the tips of their fingers and toes, their ears, their noses, and even their lips.

Rats

▲ Brown rats are 16–18 in. long, including their ropelike tail. Their fur is rough and mostly brown, speckled with black on their backs. Brown rats' bellies are gray or a creamy-white color.

Rats are one of the world's worst pests. Aggressive and highly destructive, they cause widespread damage. They eat around one fifth of the world's crops each year, pollute food, destroy electricity and telephone cables, and damage homes and properties. They also kill livestock such as chickens, ducks, and even lambs. But most dangerous of all they are known carriers of several diseases that can be fatal to humans.

▲ Like other rodents, rats have sharp front teeth that carry on growing throughout their lives. Rats constantly gnaw on hard things, such as lead pipes and cables, in order to keep their teeth short and sharp.

▼ Rats are social animals that live in large, organized colonies dominated by the largest males. When food is plentiful, for example in a granary, large numbers of rats swarm all over it to feed. They are so greedy and numerous that they consume around one fourth of the food produced by some Asian countries.

An adaptable and successful pest
The most common species of rats in Europe and North America is the brown rat, also called the Norway rat or sewer rat. It first came to Europe in the A.D. 1700s, brought from the East in sailing ships. Until then the black rat was dominant in Europe, but the brown rat was larger and more aggressive. It drove the black rat off of its territory, leaving it to live on ships and in shipyards.

The perfect habitat

Brown rats are voracious eaters and feed on anything they can find—whether it is plant, animal, or garbage. In Asia rats consume huge quantities of crops, eating millions of tons of rice and other grains each year. Rats are burrowers by nature. They build their nests under bushes or in deep burrow systems, but they are also good at climbing and can find their way into barns and warehouses where food or grain is stored. The brown rat's perfect habitat, however, is in the sewers of towns and cities. Here, deep beneath the ground, it is cool in the summer, warm in the winter, and there is a constant supply of food to eat.

Not only are rats adaptable, they are also prolific breeders. The average female rat has four to six litters each year. If she breeds all year and all of her offspring survive and mate as well, she can produce 1,000 descendants during that time.

Spreading disease

The bacteria that rats carry are much more dangerous than the rats themselves. The bubonic plague, also known as the Black Death, that spread through Europe in the A.D. 1300s, was spread by fleas carried by black rats. The fleas bit the rats, which were infected with the plague bacteria. Then the fleas bit humans, who caught the disease. The Black Death eventually killed one third of the entire population of Europe.

People have fought a constant battle against rats over the centuries. People have tried poisoning them, setting traps for them, using dogs and cats to catch them, and flooding their burrows. None of these methods has had lasting success, and the brown rat is now thought to be the most widespread mammal living on Earth.

▶ The black rat, also known as the ship rat or roof rat, is smaller and thinner than the brown rat. Its head and body measure around 8 in. Its feet and skull are a different shape than the brown rat's, and its fur is much smoother and more velvety.

SUMMARY OF CHAPTER 3: SMALL BUT DEADLY

Deadly stingers and fangs

This chapter looked at the ways in which the world's smallest creatures can be very dangerous—not only to the animals they hunt but also to any humans they may come into contact with.

Scorpions use the stingers at the ends of their tails to subdue their prey before eating it. Some scorpions, such as the Palestine yellow scorpion, have venom that can be even stronger than a cobra's. Scorpions are dangerous to people only when they sting in self-defense, either if threatened or stepped on. Unless treated quickly people can die from their stings.

Some spiders are even more dangerous. They have poisonous fangs that they sink into their prey, injecting enough venom to kill it. A few spiders, such as the Sydney funnel-web, are armed with venom powerful enough to kill humans.

Africanized honeybees—often known as killer bees—are not predators, but they are very aggressive and will sting animals or people repeatedly if their hive is threatened.

This is the ultimate self-sacrifice since, like other bees, killer bees die as a result. Each individual sting is no more powerful than that of a European honeybee, but the result of so many stings can be fatal.

Ferocious teeth

Red-bellied piranhas are said to be the fiercest fish in the world. Despite their small size, a school of piranhas can strip prey clean of all of their flesh within minutes in a feeding frenzy. However, they are aggressive and dangerous only when water levels are low and food is scarce.

Spreading disease

Many small creatures are dangerous because they spread disease. Mosquitoes, tsetse flies, and fleas can all infect people and livestock with deadly diseases. The screwworm maggot burrows under animals' skin and literally eats their flesh, causing horrible infections. Vampire bats spread a deadly disease called rabies as they move from one animal to another, sucking their blood for food. Rats carry many types of bacteria and fleas that also carry disease.

Go further . . .

 For an interactive Web site on insects, including a map of state insects and insect museums:
www.umass.edu/ent/BugNetMAP/r_state.html

Find out more about desert creatures:
www.desertusa.com

Visit the National Geographic's fun site for kids to find out about vampire bats and many of the big predators:
www.nationalgeographic.com

Nightmares of Nature by Richard Matthews (HarperCollins, 1996)

Extreme 3-D Scary Bugs by Shar Levine (Silver Dolphin Books, 2005)

 Entomologist
Person who specializes in the study of insects.

Ichthyologist
Someone who specializes in studying fish.

Conservationist
Someone who promotes the preservation of natural resources and the environment.

Epidemiologist
Person who studies epidemic diseases.

Visit the insects at San Francisco Zoo's Insect Zoo—located within the Children's Zoo—to see scorpions and goliath tarantulas.
San Francisco Zoo
San Francisco, CA 94132
Phone: (415) 753-7080
www.sfzoo.org

Surround yourself with entomology, zoology, and marine ecosystems at the National Museum of Natural History, Smithsonian Institution—featuring an IMAX theater, Discovery Room, Insect Zoo, and Naturalist Center.
National Museum of Natural History
Washington, D.C. 20560
Phone: (202) 357-2700
www.mnh.si.edu

Glossary

amphibian
An animal, such as a frog, toad, or salamander, that spends most of its life on land but has to return to water in order to breed.

antivenin
A blood serum containing antibodies that counteract the effects of an animal's venom. Antivenin is usually made from the venom it is treating.

arachnid
A member of the group of animals that includes spiders and scorpions. All arachnids have simple eyes and four pairs of legs.

bacterium (plural: bacteria)
A simple, single-celled organism that is so small it can only be seen under a microscope. Many bacteria can cause disease.

bill
A bird's beak.

bird of prey
A bird, such as an eagle or owl, that hunts and kills other animals to eat.

blubber
A thick layer of fat just beneath a sea mammal's skin that helps it keep warm and survive extremely cold temperatures.

camouflage
Coloring, patterns, or markings that help an animal blend in with its surroundings so that it is hard for either predators or prey to see it.

canine teeth
The four sharp, pointed, fanglike teeth at the front of an animal's mouth on each side of its incisors.

canopy
The part of a rain forest where, high up, the trees spread out their branches like the top of an umbrella.

carcass
The dead body of an animal.

carnivore
An animal that mostly eats meat.

colony
A group of the same type of animal, such as bats, that all live together.

crustacean
An animal with a shell such as a shrimp or a crab.

digest
To soften and break down food into very small particles that the body is able to absorb.

hippopotamuses

dominance
A position of control over others held by the strongest and most powerful animal in a group.

echolocation
The way in which some animals, such as bats, find their way around by making sounds and then using the returning echoes to locate objects.

entrails
An animal's intestines—the long tube through which food passes after leaving the stomach.

environment
An animal's or person's surroundings.

fang
A long, sharp tooth.

gizzard
A bird's second stomach, in which the food that it has eaten is ground up.

gland
A body organ that produces a particular substance such as poison.

habitat
The area where an animal lives such as grassland, sea, or rain forest.

incisors
The sharp-edged front teeth in the lower and upper jaws.

larva (plural: larvae)
An insect in the first stage of its life after it has hatched from the egg.

maggot
The larva of certain types of flies.

mammal
An animal that gives birth to live young and feeds them her own milk.

mucus
Moist, sticky slime.

musth (or must)
A period of aggressive behavior that the males of some large animals, such as elephants, go through.

muzzle
An animal's nose and mouth.

nematocyst
A tiny stinging cell on a jellyfish, sea anemone, or coral. When triggered, the cell shoots out a harpoonlike thread that injects venom into the prey or attacker.

paralyze
To make an animal or person unable to move.

parasite
A creature that is dependent on another living animal for its food. It cannot survive away from its host animal.

pellet
A small ball of undigested material that some birds, such as owls, cough up after they have eaten. An owl pellet consists mostly of bones.

pincers
The enlarged claws of animals, such as scorpions, that pinch together to catch and hold prey.

plankton
Microscopic plants and animals that float in the sea and lakes and form the basis of the food chains there.

pod
A small group of animals such as whales or seals.

polyp
A tiny creature with a tube-shaped body. Coral polyps are the small creatures whose skeletons form coral reefs after the polyps die.

predator
An animal that hunts and kills other animals to eat.

prey
Animals that are hunted and killed by other animals.

pride
A family group of lions.

proboscis
The long, tubelike mouthpart of some creatures such as cone snails and mosquitoes.

protein
A substance found in all living things, which animals need to eat in order to grow and remain healthy.

rain forest
A thick forest with very tall trees that grows in tropical countries, where it is hot all the time and rains every day.

raptor
Another name for a bird of prey such as an eagle or hawk.

reptile
A cold-blooded animal, such as a snake or crocodile, that often has scaly skin. Some reptiles lay eggs, and others give birth to live young.

retract
To pull back in.

rodent
A small mammal, such as a rat, that has large front teeth for gnawing.

great white shark

roost
A place where bats or birds rest.

saliva
The liquid in an animal's mouth that moistens food, starts breaking it down as part of the digestive process, and helps the animal swallow.

school
A large number of fish swimming together.

scute
A bony plate on the back of an animal, such as a crocodile, that makes its skin tougher and helps protect it from attack.

secrete
To produce something.

sensor
A device for detecting information about physical things such as heat, light, movement, or sound.

serrated
Having a jagged edge like the edge of a steak knife.

sheath
A close-fitting protective cover.

snout
An animal's long, projecting nose.

species
A particular type of animal or plant.

talons
The long, sharp, curved claws of a bird of prey.

tentacle
A long, flexible, armlike part of the body of certain animals, such as octopuses, that is used both for movement and grasping things.

territory
The area in which an animal lives and hunts for its food.

toxic
Poisonous or caused by poisons.

toxin
A poisonous substance—especially one formed in the body.

translucent
Allowing some light to shine through but not transparent or completely see-through.

tropical
To do with the regions known as the tropics—parts of the world on each side of the equator where it is usually hot.

venom
The poisonous fluid made by some animals such as snakes, scorpions, and spiders.

virus
A microscopic organism that multiplies inside the body cells of a host animal. Viruses spread easily and many of them cause diseases.

Index

Acknowledgments

The publisher would like to thank the following for permission to reproduce their material. Every care has been taken to trace copyright holders. However, if there have been unintentional omissions or failure to trace copyright holders, we apologize and will, if informed, endeavor to make corrections in any future edition.

Key: b = bottom, c = center, l = left, r = right, t = top

1 Oxford Scientific Films (OSF); 4 Getty Images; 7 Getty Images; 8 Natural History Picture Agency (NHPA); 9 Steve Bloom; 10*tl* Getty Images; 10–11 Steve Bloom; 11*br* Steve Bloom; 12*tl* NHPA; 12*br* Steve Bloom; 13 NHPA; 14*bl* Steve Bloom; 14–15*tr* NHPA; 15*br* Getty Images; 16*tl* Nature Picture Library (Nature); 16*tr* Corbis; 16–17*cb* Steve Bloom; 17*cl* Steve Bloom; 18*bl* Still Pictures; 19*tl* Steve Bloom; 19*br* Ardea; 20*tl* NHPA; 20*b* OSF; 21*t* Getty Images; 22–23 Steve Bloom; 22*b* OSF; 23*t* Corbis; 24 NHPA; 25 Corbis; 26 Frank Lane Picture Agency; 27 Getty Images; 28*t* National Geographic Image Collection; 28*b* Corbis; 29*t* NHPA; 29*b* Corbis; 32*tl* Nature; 32–33 Getty Images; 33*t* Nature; 33*b* Nature; 34*tl* Getty Images; 34*tr* Ardea; 34–35 Ardea; 36*tl* Corbis; 36*tr* Corbis; 36*bl* Corbis; 37*c* NHPA; 37*br* Nature; 38*b* Ardea; 39*t* Frank Lane Picture Agency; 39*b* Corbis; 40 Corbis; 41 Alamy; 42 NHPA; 43 Corbis; 44*t* NHPA; 44*b* NHPA; 45*t* NHPA; 45*c* NHPA; 45*cb* OSF; 46–47 OSF; 47*br* NHPA; 48*tl* OSF; 48–49*c* Corbis; 48–49*b* OSF; 49*t* Corbis; 50*t* OSF; 51*tr* Ardea; 51*b* OSF; 52*tl* Corbis; 52*cl* Corbis; 52*bl* Corbis; 52–53 Corbis; 53*tr* Corbis; 54*t* Science Photo Library (SPL); 54*b* Ardea; 55*t* Still Pictures; 56*tl* Nature; 56*tr* Ardea; 56*b* OSF; 57 SPL; 59 Steve Bloom; 59 Corbis; 64 Steve Bloom

The publisher would like to thank the following illustrators:
10–11 cheetah skeleton/Tom Connell; 16 chimp attack diagram/Mike Davis; 23 shark attack diagram/Mike Davis; 30–31 snake heads/Jurgen Ziewe; 36 stinger diagram/Mike Davis; 39 stinger diagram/Mike Davis; 45 spider nest art/Mike Davis; 46 scorpion art/Mike Davis; 50 stinger diagram/Mike Davis